Food Culture:
Celebrating
Diverse Traditions

KRISTIN PETRIE MS, RD
ABDO Publishing Company

visit us at
www.abdopublishing.com

Published by ABDO Publishing Company, 8000 West 78th Street, Edina, Minnesota 55439.
Copyright © 2012 by Abdo Consulting Group, Inc. International copyrights reserved in all
countries. No part of this book may be reproduced in any form without written permission from the
publisher. The Checkerboard Library™ is a trademark and logo of ABDO Publishing Company.

Printed in the United States of America, North Mankato, Minnesota.
062011
092011

 PRINTED ON RECYCLED PAPER

Cover Photos: Getty Images, iStockphoto
Interior Photos: Alamy pp. 15, 26; AP Images pp. 5, 7; Corbis pp. 24, 25;
     Getty Images pp. 11, 13, 23, 27, 29; iStockphoto pp. 1, 9, 18;
     Photolibrary pp. 8, 10, 12, 14, 17, 19, 21

Series Coordinator: BreAnn Rumsch
Editors: Megan M. Gunderson, BreAnn Rumsch
Art Direction: Neil Klinepier

Library of Congress Cataloging-in-Publication Data

Petrie, Kristin, 1970-
 Food culture : celebrating diverse traditions / Kristin Petrie.
    p. cm. -- (Mission: Nutrition)
 Includes index.
 ISBN 978-1-61783-083-9
 1. Food habits--Juvenile literature. I. Title.
 GT2850.P48 2012
 394.1'2--dc22
                          2011010413

Contents

Food Is Culture

Picture a turkey with stuffing on Thanksgiving Day. Imagine some apple pie with ice cream on the Fourth of July. Think of a birthday cake loaded with candles. Are these familiar holiday and celebration foods for your family?

Have you ever wondered why people eat turkey for Thanksgiving dinner? Do you know why Americans put candles on their birthday cakes? After all, lighting a cake on fire might seem odd to someone from Nigeria or Nepal. And why do you make a wish before blowing out the candles?

These celebration foods are for special occasions. What about the everyday foods you choose? Cereal and bagels may be your usual breakfast foods. But in Japan, a traditional breakfast includes rice, fish, and seaweed! Do you normally eat a sandwich for lunch? For Brazilians, that's just a snack. A five-course meal is their midday tradition.

One of the ways cultural groups identify themselves is by the foods they eat.

The foods you eat daily and for special occasions are part of your **culture**. This is formed by many factors, including your **ethnicity**, community, and religion. Keep reading! You will learn about foods, folklore, and **customs** from around the world.

Borrowed Meals

What is your family's favorite meal? Is it steak and potatoes or spaghetti with meatballs? Favorite foods vary widely across the globe. What you eat is part of your food **culture**.

There may be several cultural groups where you live. Each has its own food practices. For hundreds of years, people from many nations have settled in North America. They have brought their traditions with them. As a result, the United States has been called the world's cultural "melting pot" or "salad bowl."

All these different traditions have contributed to the varied food culture of the United States. This means most foods eaten by Americans came from other countries! Pancakes and waffles were created by the Dutch. Today, these foods are American breakfast favorites. And the hot dog was invented in Germany. But today, this handheld food is a must at American baseball games.

Even meatloaf was not made up in the United States. Dishes of chopped meat go all the way back to ancient Rome! Today's familiar meat, bread, and vegetable mixture grew popular

Chew On This

In space, eating food is based on science more than culture. Applesauce squeezed from a tube was the first food eaten there. Astronaut John Glenn was the lucky guy to try it out.

during the **Great Depression**. Poor families stretched their small meat supply by mixing it with other ingredients. So today, meatloaf represents part of America's history.

The hot dog began as the frankfurter. This word simply means "a sausage from Frankfurt."

The New World

Throughout the **New World**, foods are as varied as the regions they are found in. In North America, cooking styles reflect different people's backgrounds.

In northwestern Canada, many dishes feature caribou meat. Meanwhile, a sweet butter tart and a meat pie known as Tourtière are prepared in southeastern Canada.

Along US coasts, traditional meals are based on fresh seafood. New England is famous for its chowders, while the Pacific Northwest is known for its salmon.

Meanwhile, traditional Southern meals often feature biscuits, fried chicken, and collard greens. The Southwest showcases its tamales and enchiladas. And in Mexico, meals are rarely served without corn tortillas and black beans.

Cooking traditions are passed from one generation to the next.

Feijoada completa *is the national dish of Brazil.*

Traditional Central and South American cooking reflects an interesting history. People cook with native foods as well as foods introduced by European explorers. They commonly use corn, beans, tropical fruits, wheat, beef, and chicken. Each **culture**'s cooking style uses these ingredients in different ways.

For example, *carbonada criolla* is a rich stew of beef and squash eaten in Argentina. In Brazil, *Feijoada completa* features cooked meats served with greens, beans, rice, and sauces.

Chile, Colombia, and Venezuela enjoy traditional fish and vegetable stews. The Venezuelan version is called *sancocho*. It includes chunks of pumpkin.

Wonder Food

In Japan today, the average person eats 132 pounds (60 kg) of rice each year.

Rice is the **staple** food of about one-half of the world's population. Asia is the largest continent on Earth. Countless **cultures** and cooking styles exist there. Yet one food is common to them all. You guessed it, rice!

People in China and Thailand start their day with this important food. Breakfast is often a rice porridge called congee. In China, people even greet each other by asking, "Have you had rice today?" This is similar to the English greeting "How are you?"

Bahn cuon are commonly eaten in Vietnam. These steamed rice dumplings are filled with pork, shrimp, mushrooms, and onions.

Pho is a filling soup of broth, rice noodles, meat, and vegetables.

People in Japan eat five times more fish than those in the United States do! Even so, traditional Japanese meals are based on rice. Rice is served separately from other dishes. These include vegetables, clear soup, noodles, fish, tofu, and meat. Rice is also used for sushi.

In India, rice is prepared in countless ways. It is pressed, puffed, baked, beaten, and ground up! Rice is often served with meat, vegetables, and spices.

Vast Variety

In European countries, favorite meals range from very heavy to quite light. Sausage, sauerkraut, and potatoes are popular with Germans. In Ireland, a common dish is a big plate of mashed potatoes with butter called *champ*. Traditional Polish meals feature pierogi. These doughy pockets are filled with meat, potatoes, or vegetables.

Various parts of Europe are known for their local sausages.

Along the Mediterranean Sea, people prefer lighter foods. Fish, vegetables, cheese, bread, nuts, and olives are featured in their diets. Moussaka is a well-known Greek dish that includes meat as well as eggplant.

Many Middle Eastern people are Muslims. They eat only with the right hand because they consider the left hand unclean.

The **Middle East** is divided among many nations. So, many cooking styles are found there. *Hashwa* combines rice, lamb, pine nuts, and cinnamon. The mixture is stuffed into leaves, vegetables, or other meats. Another lamb mixture known as kibbe includes wheat. It can be eaten as a dip for bread, a baked loaf, or meatballs in soup.

Plenty of foods are eaten across the entire region. Baba ghanoush is a popular eggplant dip. *Sfeena* are meat pies, and *mansaf* is a bread layered with rice and lamb. *Yukhee* is a tasty stew made of tomatoes and other vegetables.

Mixed Tradition

Africa also features a great range of **cultural** groups, history, and foods. Three-fourths of Africa's population lives in rural areas. These people hold tightly to **staple** foods such as yams, plantains, and cassava. Meat is rarely eaten. Instead, beans and lentils provide the **protein** people need.

Cassava and other plant foods make up the main diet of rural Africans.

In contrast, populations of East Africa were influenced by European settlers. These settlers brought corn, fine cheeses, and beef to the area.

East Africans value cows, goats, and sheep. But the milk and wool are worth more than the meat these animals can provide. So most people here remain **vegetarians**. They often enjoy *nhopi dovi*, a dish made with mashed pumpkin and peanuts.

Long ago, the southern end of Africa was the perfect stop for explorers. For this reason, the cooking style there combines European, Indian, and African foods. A typical dish called *bobotie* shows this blend.

Bobotie mixes ground lamb, bread, lemon juice, and chopped apples and almonds. Curry and other seasonings flavor the recipe. A custard of milk and egg top off this traditional dish.

Bobotie *is a South African favorite!*

Food Folklore

Nearly every **culture** has its own collection of folklore. It includes the beliefs, stories, and traditions passed among a group of people. Much of it relates to food!

For example, a Greek myth helps explain why the land doesn't always produce food. The story features Demeter, the Greek goddess of agriculture. Hades, the god of the dead, took her daughter Persephone to the underworld. The goddess searched everywhere but could not find Persephone. Sad without her child, Demeter lost interest in helping the plants grow.

Eventually, the Greek god Zeus ordered Hades to return Persephone. When Demeter was reunited with her daughter, everything started to grow again. One problem remained. While in the underworld, Persephone had eaten pomegranate seeds. This tied her to a marriage with Hades.

Luckily, Zeus arranged for Demeter and Hades to share Persephone. Persephone returned to the underworld for four months every year. During that time, her mother was sad and

*Greek farmers used the tale of Persephone
and Demeter to understand the harvest cycle.*

the land would grow **dormant**. But when Persephone returned to the goddess, the land would grow fertile once again!

Some folklore is based on history. In the 1800s, there was a young man named John. John liked apples so much that he planted orchards throughout Ohio and Indiana. He also gave apple seeds to everyone he met. Who was that young apple lover? Today, Americans know him as Johnny Appleseed!

Stories like these are fun. Yet, folklore can also offer helpful tips about food. Ancient

You've probably heard that "an apple a day keeps the doctor away." It's because apples have lots of vitamins!

In Japanese culture, eating lobster promises long life.

Romans thought apples had magical powers. And long ago, some **cultures** believed garlic could keep away evil. Today we know both of these foods do help you stay healthy.

Sometimes folklore develops into food traditions. Japanese people eat red foods for luck. And for the New Year, they eat seaweed for long life. In the **Middle East**, sugared almonds are served at weddings to guarantee sweetness in life. And in India, sweets represent wealth.

Many Americans say chicken soup cures the common cold. So, bringing someone soup when they are sick is a kind practice. This old remedy may not actually cure the illness. However, the soup's heat and steam can relieve a stuffy nose. In addition, soup is comforting to eat. What a nice tradition!

We know all these tales and tips because they were passed down to us. Some may be helpful and some may be silly! Either way, passing down these stories helps preserve your **unique** traditions.

Celebrate!

What do Halloween, Thanksgiving, Hanukkah, Kwanzaa, and Christmas all have in common? Food! Eating is a central part of many celebrations.

Some celebrations take place on a large scale. Mardi Gras is a famous festival of food and fun. It takes place around the world. Also known as Fat Tuesday, it falls on the day before Lent begins. Lent is a long period of prayer and **fasting** for Christians.

Louisiana is well known for its **unique** Mardi Gras celebration. There, serving King cake is an important food tradition. The cake is a ring-shaped, sweetened bread. A small token is hidden inside. The person who finds it is expected to serve the following year's King cake.

Each year, the people of Buñol, Spain, hold a very unusual festival. It is known as La Tomatina, and it is all about tomatoes. On the last Wednesday of August, thousands of people come to have a food fight! Their only goal is to cover one another with

La Tomatina participants throw more than 110 tons (100 t) of tomatoes in the streets of Buñol.

slimy tomato guts. Why did this tradition start? No one really knows, but they have a lot of fun!

In the fall, many children look forward to celebrating Halloween. That is because this fun holiday means getting lots of candy! When it's dark, trick-or-treaters go out in costume to collect sweets from their neighbors.

Some holidays are celebrated with loved ones. In the United States, celebrating Thanksgiving Day dates back to 1621. In the spring after their first hard winter, the Pilgrims at Plymouth Colony learned to plant corn. A Native American named Tisquantum showed them how.

That fall, the settlers celebrated the corn harvest and their survival. They invited the local Native Americans to join them. This was the first Thanksgiving.

Today, corn stalk decorations and a large turkey serve as symbols of the beginning of American **culture**. People celebrate this holiday each November. Canadians celebrate a similar Thanksgiving Day in October. The first took place in Newfoundland in 1578.

Many cultures celebrate holidays at the end of the year. These include Christmas and Hanukkah. From December 26 to January 1, African Americans celebrate Kwanzaa. They honor their ancestors and celebrate their **ethnicity**.

At the end of Kwanzaa, *karamu* is served. There is no set menu for this feast. Families may enjoy traditional recipes from any African country. Peanut soup, *jollof* rice, and okra and greens are just some of the dishes people might prepare.

The name **Kwanzaa** *comes from a Swahili phrase that means "first fruits."*

How We Eat

We've traveled the globe and discovered many different kinds of food. You may have even worked up a good appetite! But how do you get your food to your mouth? Do you use forks, spoons, and knives? Do you prefer chopsticks? Or do you simply use your hands?

The way you eat is another important part of your food **culture**. People from industrial countries such as the United States usually use silverware. Forks, spoons, and knives pierce, scoop, and cut food.

In Eastern cultures and developing nations, people eat much differently. Chinese, Japanese, and other Asian

Making injera *is a key part of preparing a meal in Ethiopia.*

Chapatis are one of the oldest foods in the world.

people use chopsticks as their eating tools. And in other parts of the world, people may simply use their hands. In fact, this is the most common eating practice.

Sometimes food itself is used as an eating tool! In Ethiopia, a large, thin pancake called *injera* may cover an entire table. It is mounded with food. Diners tear the pancake and use it to scoop bitefuls of the feast.

A smaller version of this method exists in India. There, people use round, flat breads called chapatis to scoop up vegetables or spicy sauces.

When you think about it, eating with your hands makes a lot of sense. People who use silverware still eat many foods with their hands. You probably eat hamburgers, pizza, gyros, and tacos with your hands. Whatever the occasion or method, eating food is a delicious way to experience **culture**!

A Healthier You

Have you ever felt sleepy after Thanksgiving dinner or sick after eating too many holiday sweets? At the holidays and other celebrations, it can be hard to eat healthily. But the *Let's Move!* program can help. Follow these tips to stay on track during your next special meal.

WATCH YOUR PORTION SIZES! Eat smaller amounts of different dishes so you can taste more without overeating.

GET MOVING! Take a walk as a family after your big meal. You'll feel better and get to enjoy spending time together.

FAST SAFELY! Be sure not to use fasting as a dieting method. If you want to fast as part of your religious beliefs, talk with a parent or guardian first. He or she can help make sure you still get the nutrition you need to feel healthy during your fast.

Let's Move!

For more information, check out *Let's Move!* online at **www.letsmove.gov**.

Let's Move! is a campaign started by First Lady Michelle Obama to raise a healthier generation of kids and combat childhood obesity. This movement works to provide schools, families, and communities with the tools to help kids be more active, eat better, and live healthfully.

The *Let's Move!* Web site provides information about the movement. It includes recipes as well as helpful tips on nutrition and physical activity. And, there are action tools to promote healthier foods in your local schools or start a *Let's Move!* Meetup.

MIX IT UP! Being open to trying a new spin on an old favorite can make a traditional meal feel fresh as well as guilt-free. Try trading:

- butter for chicken broth or olive oil
- flour tortillas for corn tortillas
- fried vegetables for steamed vegetables
- mashed russet potatoes for baked sweet potatoes
- white bread for whole wheat bread
- white rice for brown rice

Glossary

culture - the customs, arts, and tools of a nation or a people at a certain time. Something relating to culture is cultural.

custom - a practice common to a group or a place.

dormant - not active but able to become active.

ethnicity - the relation to a group of people based on a common race, nationality, religion, or culture.

fast - to go without food.

Great Depression - the period from 1929 to 1942 of worldwide economic trouble. There was little buying or selling, and many people could not find work.

Middle East - a region made up of the lands of southwestern Asia and northeastern Africa.

New World - the continents of the western half of Earth.

protein - a substance which provides energy to the body and serves as a major class of foods for animals. Foods high in protein include cheese, eggs, fish, meat, and milk.

staple - something used, needed, or enjoyed constantly, usually by many people.

unique - being the only one of its kind.

vegetarian - one who lives on a diet consisting mostly of plant foods and sometimes eggs or dairy products. Vegetarians do not eat meat, poultry, or fish.

To learn more about celebrating diverse traditions, visit ABDO Publishing Company online. Web sites about food culture are featured on our Book Links page. These links are routinely monitored and updated to provide the most current information available.
www.abdopublishing.com

Index